SMART BRAIN RIGHT BRAIN

Tales of Inventions

Om KIDZ
An imprint of Om Books International

First Published in 2021 by

Om Books International

Corporate & Editorial Office
A-12, Sector 64, Noida 201 301
Uttar Pradesh, India
Phone: +91 120 477 4100
Email: editorial@ombooks.com
Website: www.ombooksinternational.com

Sales Office
107, Ansari Road, Darya Ganj
New Delhi 110 002, India
Phone: +91 11 4000 9000
Email: sales@ombooks.com

Author: Shweta Sinha
Editor: Kirti Pathak
Art & Design: Anshuman Pandey, Gaurav Bhandari, Harish Arya

ISBN: 978-93-5276-836-3

Printed in India

10 9 8 7 6 5 4 3 2 1

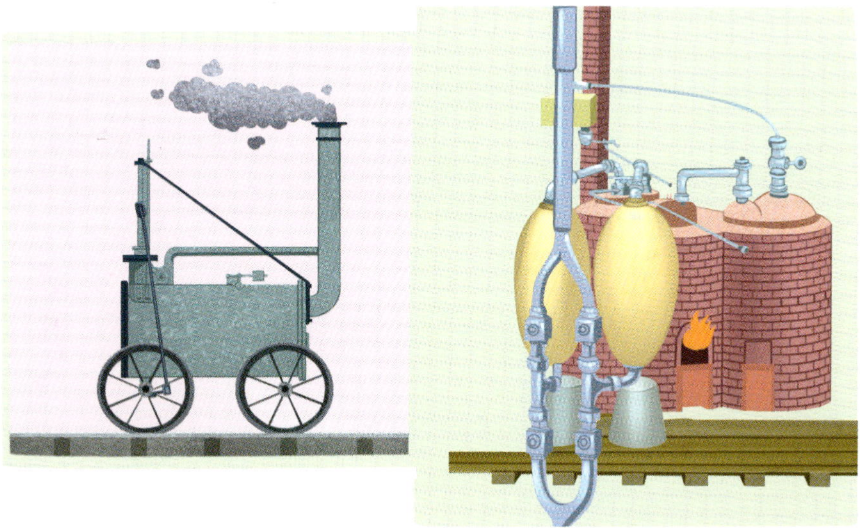

CONTENTS

1. What Is an Invention?

An **invention** is a completely new thing that someone creates. When we invent something, it lets us do stuff we could not do before. Or, it makes our job easier or faster to do.

Some inventions have changed the way we live.

About 5,000 years ago, people walked, or rode on animal backs to get around. The invention of the **wheel** changed the way people travelled.

POCKET FACT

We have used wheels for thousands of years, but no one knows who first created it.

They built carts and carriages with wheels. Without wheels, there would be no cars, trucks or even bicycles!

The **light bulb** is another great invention. People in the old days burnt oil lamps and candles for light.

Many scientists worked on producing the light bulb. Finally, in 1879, Thomas Alva Edison came up with a usable design. Today, we cannot imagine a life without light bulbs.

Thomas Alva Edison

DID YOU KNOW?

The wheel, the spear, the knife and the arrow are some of the earliest inventions.

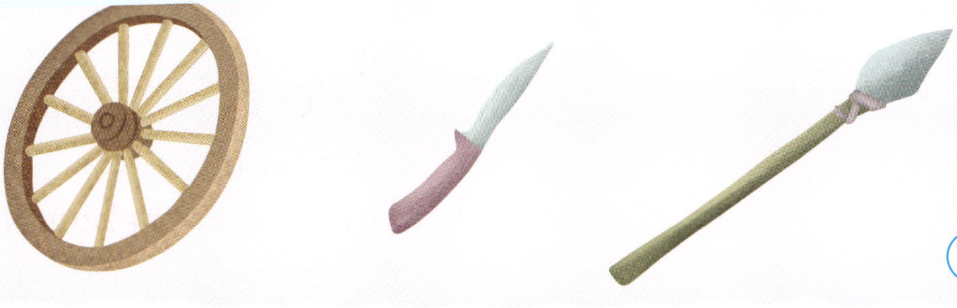

2. Inventions in Travel

For centuries people have invented ways to make travelling easier and faster.

Bicycle

A **bicycle** is a simple travel machine. Yet, it took many years and many inventors to get it right. The first bicycle had no pedals. It was simply two wheels on a wooden frame. You had to push along the ground to get it moving.

Rolling the bicycle down a slope was a fun sport during those days.

POCKET FACT

The first bicycle built around 1790 was named 'celerifere'.

Steam Locomotive

The first **steam locomotive** chugged out in 1804. At first, the locomotives were used to transport goods. By the 1850s people started travelling in them too. Even today, locomotive trains are a popular mode of transport.

In 1698, Thomas Savery first thought of a steam engine. James Watt improved the design and made it useful.

DID YOU KNOW?

In the beginning, people were really scared of the speed of those early trains.

Car

Initially, people tried to build cars by joining a steam engine to a horse carriage. This idea failed. The steam engine was just too bulky for the roads.

In 1876, Nikolaus Otto invented a much smaller engine. Karl Benz then used the engine to build the world's first car in 1885. He called the car, 'Motorwagen'.

The Benz Motorwagen on a stamp issued by Germany

Nicholaus Otto

Karl Benz

DID YOU KNOW? The first cars were called 'horse-less carriages' as they were mostly horse carts fitted with engines.

Cars took a few more years to become popular. In 1908, Henry Ford introduced the Model T car. Model T was sturdy and easy to drive. It remained the most popular car for several years.

The Model T had to be started by cranking a handle in front of the car.

Henry Ford

POCKET FACT

The steam locomotives ran on coal while cars ran on petrol.

Taking to the Skies

People have always wanted to fly like birds.

In the 1780s, people took to the skies in **hot air balloons**. The hot air balloon was invented by the Montgolfier brothers from France.

Next, people tried to fly in **gliders**. George Cayley built the first glider in 1853. Later, Otto Lilienthal designed a series of gliders. But gliders did not stay in the air for long.

DID YOU KNOW?

The world's first air passengers were a duck, a sheep and a rooster. They flew in a hot air balloon.

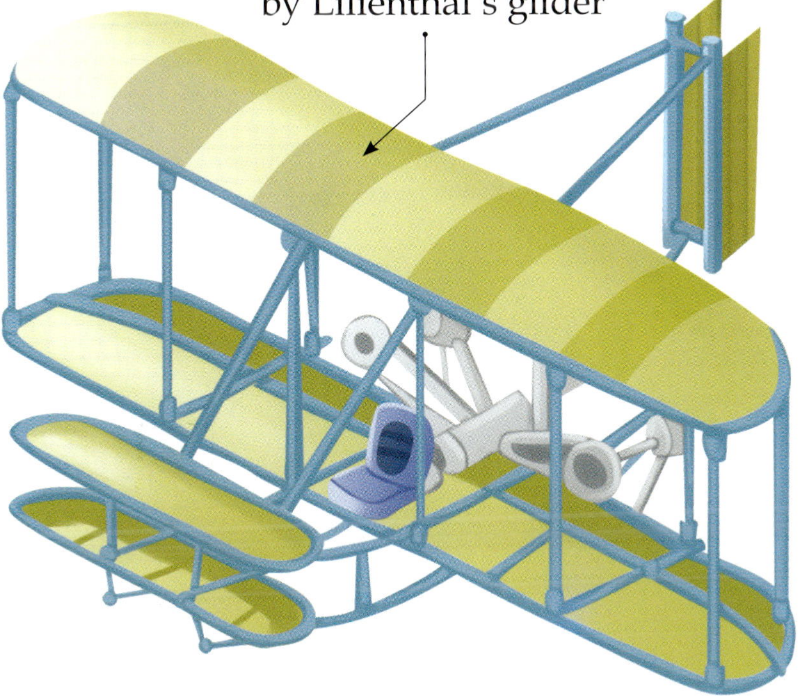

Orville and Wilbur Wright were two American brothers. They invented the engine-powered flying machine. In 1903, Orville made the world's first successful **aeroplane** flight.

Today, high-speed jet liners swiftly carry us from place to place.

POCKET FACT

The first flight rose only 9 feet - about as high as a room's ceiling.

3. Inventions in Media

Do you enjoy listening to music and watching movies? You can thank Thomas Alva Edison for giving us both.

Phonograph

In the early days, the only way to enjoy music was by listening to live musicians. In 1877, Edison found a way to record and play sounds. He invented the **phonograph**.

'Mary had a little lamb' was the first song ever to be recorded on the phonograph.

Today you can record any sound you want to. You can play music on lots of devices .

Thomas Alva Edison

POCKET FACT

Edison invented the phonograph and electric light bulb in his famous laboratory in Menlo Park. He soon became known as the "Wizard of Menlo Park".

First Movie Player

In 1891, Thomas Edison invented the motion-picture player. He called it the **kinetoscope**. A kinetoscope was a box with a strip of pictures. It had a peephole to look inside. When the strip was pulled through the box, it seemed like the pictures were moving.

DID YOU KNOW?

People paid a nickel to watch the first short movie on the kinetoscope in 1894.

4. Inventions in Communications

Telephone

In 1876, Alexander Graham Bell invented the **telephone**. The telephone completely changed the way we communicated. It became possible to talk to someone far away.

Alexander Graham Bell

DID YOU KNOW?

The US President, Rutherford B. Hayes was amazed by the telephone, but didn't think it was a useful invention.

The early telephones were only meant for talking.

Mobile phones allowed people to send text messages as well.

Today's **smartphones** let us call, send texts, click pictures, play music and do much more.
IBM launched the first smartphone in 1994.

Steve Jobs

POCKET FACT

Steve Jobs played an important role in developing the modern smartphone.

Television

In 1926, John Baird presented the first **television** to the public. He had built his crude machine with everyday objects including cookie tins and bicycle lights.

John Baird

Baird successfully transmitted the first pictures, but they were too fuzzy. People didn't quite like the fuzzy pictures. So Baird's model was never used.

POCKET FACT

The early television built by Baird was called the Tin Stove Televisor.

In 1927, Philo Farnsworth built the first electrical television. Some years later, Vladimir Zworykin, improved upon the design. The modern television has been built on their designs.

Philo Farnsworth

The early televisions were basically a big box with a small screen. In comparison, today's televisions are much slimmer with large screens.

DID YOU KNOW?

At first, televisions showed only black and white pictures. Colour televisions did not come out until 1953.

5. The Age of Computers

The computer is really a clever device. It helps us easily do lots of tasks. But computers haven't been around for very long.

In the 1820s, Charles Babbage designed machines to do math calculations. These machines were later used to build computers.

Charles Babbage

The first working computer, Z3, was built in 1941. Z3 was as big as a large room. Its inventor was Konrad Zuse, a German engineer.

POCKET FACT

Small, modern computers were developed only in the 1970s.

Internet

The **internet** is amazing. It lets you send messages, make calls, play games and do so much more. But, who invented the internet?

A team of scientists, engineers and programmers developed the internet. In the 1960s, they connected a few computers to each other with wires.

This created a small network of computers. Slowly, more computers got connected to the network. Soon, this small network grew to become the internet we use today.

DID YOU KNOW?

Over a billion people worldwide use the internet every day.

6. Inventions in Food

Chocolate, Yum!

Who doesn't love chocolates? But do you know how they came about?

Chocolate is made from the cacao beans that grow in South America and Africa. Nearly 2,500 years ago, the Mayan and Aztec people of Mexico made a frothy, bitter drink called 'chocol haa'. The rest of the world had not yet heard of cacao.

DID YOU KNOW?

Cacao beans were precious to the Mayans and Aztecs. They used the beans like money.

In the 1500s, the Spanish people invaded Mexico. They brought the cacao beans to Europe. There they tried to make the 'chocol haa' drink too. The Spaniards turned the drink sweet by adding sugar to it.

In 1846, J.S. Fry tried a new recipe. He replaced the water in the drink with cocoa butter. He let the paste cool in moulds. Voila! Fry created the world's first chocolate bar.

POCKET FACT

Daniel Peter and Henri Nestlé set up the Nestlé company that made milk chocolates popular.

Ice-cream for all

Once upon a time only kings and queens ate icecream. This was because icecreams were hard and expensive to make as freezers had not been invented.

In 1843, Nancy Johnson invented an easy way to make icecreams. Her icecream maker was a simple machine with a handle. When the handle was cranked, it froze the icecream mix inside. Now everyone could enjoy icecreams.

DID YOU KNOW?

Refrigerators for home use were invented only in 1913.

7. Inventions for Doctors

Thermometer

What is one of the first things a doctor does when you fall sick? They stick a **thermometer** in your mouth to take your temperature. Gabriel Fahrenheit first invented the thermometer in 1714. His thermometer used a liquid called mercury. Most modern thermometers are digital and do not use mercury anymore.

POCKET FACT

An oral thermometer is placed under the tongue to measure temperature.

Counting Heartbeats

Like the thermometer, a **stethoscope** is a doctor's essential tool. It lets them check for problems by listening to the patient's heartbeat and breathing.

In 1816, a French doctor René Laënnec, invented the first stethoscope. It was a simple wooden tube that picked up sounds and made it louder. Modern stethoscopes have a diaphragm that amplifies the sound before it reaches the doctor's ears.

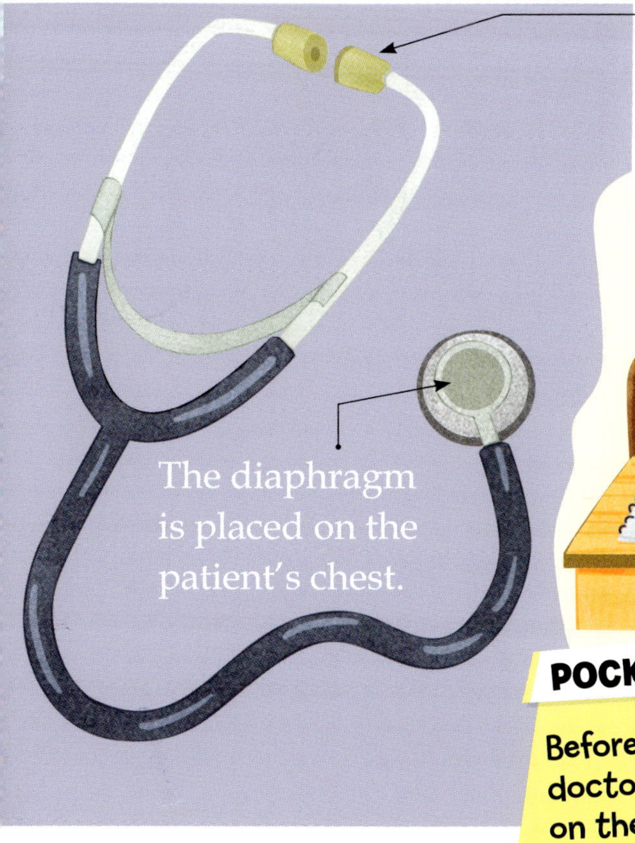

POCKET FACT

Before there were stethoscopes, doctors placed their ear directly on the patient's chest.

Syringe

The **syringe** is a tube with a hollow needle. It is used to inject medicines into a patient's body. A syringe is another necessary device in a doctor's kit.

The syringe was first invented by Francis Rynd, an Irish doctor, in 1844. The first syringes were made of metal or glass. Today we use disposable or single-use plastic syringes. They were invented by a veterinarian, Colin Murdoch, in 1956.

DID YOU KNOW? 'Hypodermic needle' is another name given to a syringe.

8. Invention vs. Discovery

Discovery is something which already exists. It remains unknown to us until someone finds out about it. Discoveries often lead to inventions.

Electricity was a discovery. It always existed around us. A bolt of lightning is a form of electricity.

Two hundred years ago, a man called Benjamin Franklin studied electricity. His discoveries led to several inventions such as these:

- Electric light bulb.
- Television.
- Computers.
- All electrical appliances like microwaves, blenders, hair dryers, etc.

POCKET FACT

The discovery of rubber led to the invention of tyres.

Who invented it?

Match the invention to the inventor:

Phonograph 	 J.S. Fry
Aeroplane 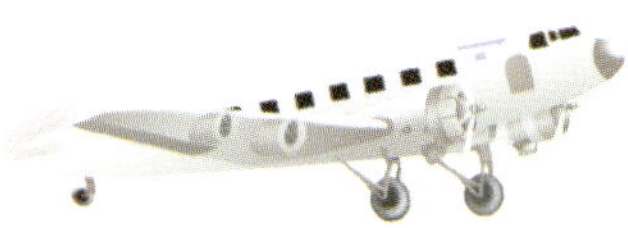	 Alexander Graham Bell
Chocolate bar 	 Orville and Wilbur Wright
Model T car 	 Thomas Edison
Telephone 	 Henry Ford

True or False

Jim thinks he knows all. He shows off his knowledge to his little sister, Joan. Can you guess which statement of Jim is correct and which is not?

1. A syringe is used to inject medicines. (True/False)
2. People have been riding bicycles for thousands of years. (True/False)
3. Gabriel Fahrenheit invented the mercury thermometer. (True/False)
4. Rubber was invented. (True/False)
5. A team of engineers, scientists and programmers developed the internet. (True/False)

Inventions

Circle the things that you think were invented by someone.

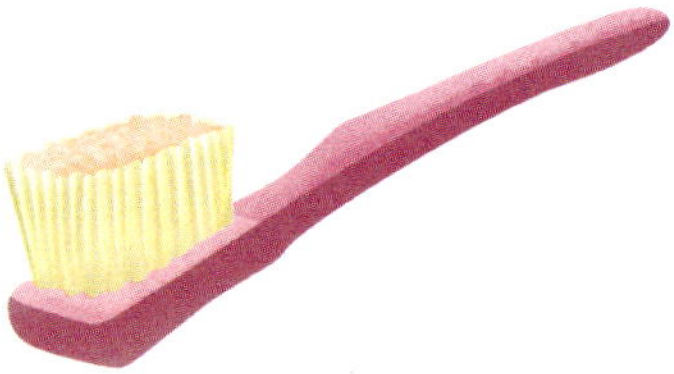

toothbrush

rock

television

mobile phone

bicycle

insect

potato

computer

sun

Hint: Every manmade thing is an invention.